Rule of Thumb

A Guide to
Small Business Marketing

David Catalan

Published by

WriteLife   Rule of Thumb
(An imprint of Boutique of Quality
Books Publishing Company)   http://ruleofthumbbiz.com

www.writelife.com

Printed in the United States of America

ISBN 978-1-60808-047-2 (p)

ISBN 978-1-60808-101-1 (e)

First Edition

Contents

Why Rule of Thumb?

This book is part of the Rule of Thumb series produced in affiliation with the Rule of Thumb for Business whose mission is to "enrich business growth and development." The Rule of Thumb series offers basic information in plain language that will help you start, grow and sustain your business. The explanation for using the *"rule of thumb"* concept was introduced in the first book and is included again here.

Throughout history, a *"rule of thumb"* was used in measurements in a wide variety of businesses and vocations. The following list gives a few examples of how the thumb was used for measuring:

- In agriculture, the thumb was used to measure the depth at which to plant a seed.
- In restaurants and pubs, the thumb was used to measure the temperature of beer and ale.
- Tailors used the thumb to make sure enough space was allowed between the person's skin and his/her clothing. For example, the space between the cuff of the sleeve and the wrist had to be at least the width of the thumb.

- Carpenters used the width of the thumb rather than a ruler for measuring. For example, a notch in a board may need to be cut two thumb widths from the edge.

A *"rule of thumb"* is an idea or rule that may be applied in most situations, but not all. The *"rules of thumb"* in this book give you many reliable, convenient and simple rules that will help you remember many "dos" and "don'ts" that go with owning and running a business. Many of these concepts can also be used in a variety of business situations ranging from management, sales, customer service, human resources and leadership. The information is designed to be easy, simple and action-oriented. To learn more about the Rule of Thumb for Business organization visit our website at www.ruleofthumbbiz.com. – *Rule of Thumb for Business.*

Chapter 1
What is Marketing?

All of us go to market on a regular basis. Why? Well, we go to the grocery store to buy what we need, what we think we need, and for a sense of adventure to see what is new and what bargains we may find in the product-laden aisles. A television commercial that shows a family at breakfast triggers the need for cereal and milk. The morning newspaper that features a discount ad for Pepsi triggers the need for a Pepsi™. Enroute to the shopping mall, a billboard that advertises Omaha Steaks® on sale for a limited time triggers another need. At the checkout stand, the short trip to the store for only cereal and milk yields four grocery bags filled with family favorites and new items to try—a result of *impulse buying*, a normal human response to the successful *marketing concepts* created by retailers, distributors, and manufacturers of consumer goods. Such concepts are created and then displayed at outlets in attractive and convenient places, sending the message: "Buy ME."

Instead of heating up soup and making sandwiches at home during lunchtime, it is more convenient to grab the kids and go to McDonald's. Besides, the kids are collecting the latest movie souvenirs given out by McDonald's, reminding Dad that a weekend visit to the multiplex cinema is on the calendar to see Harry Potter and his two faithful friends once more triumph over evil. Yes, one visit to McDonald's produces multiple responses to the power of marketing.

***

Is this marketing? You bet, it is! And it is the most fundamental type, targeting the family and inviting everyone to buy the end product. **Marketing is all around us**: from the furnishings in our homes to the clothes we wear, from the car we drive to the fuel that goes into the tank, from the books and magazines we read to the movies we see, from our career needs to planning for retirement. The people impacted by marketing are called *customers*, and it is the goal of good marketing to identify, recruit, and keep customers. Small business owners can understand the marketing process by focusing on the basics, or what is commonly referred to as "the four Ps" plus one.

The traditional Ps:

- *Product:* the goods or services that you market and sell.
- *Price:* the value of the goods or services expressed in dollars.
- *Promotion:* the method of communicating the goods and services.

- *Place:* the strategy for getting products into the buyers' hands.

The new marketing P:

- *Position:* the way the product is imagined in the mind of the buyer.

These five Ps are the marketing mix that attracts and engages the consumer, resulting in a sale. Whether the product is beer, toothpaste, or a new home, all of the ingredients must be considered or the marketing cake you are baking will fall flat and fail.

Step through the doorway of your home or office and observe: the ads on the sides of city buses, the murals on exterior building walls, the signs in retail store windows, supermarket bulletin boards, posters along airport concourses, people distributing fliers on street corners, and the occasional skywriting. Yes, all marketing and all with the one goal of making a sale!

However, you should not limit yourself to marketing which exists by calling attention to available products or services—Be Creative! Beyond what is lies what could be, or, as better said by George Bernard Shaw, one of England's great playwrights, "You see things, and say, 'Why' But I dream things that never were; and I say, 'Why not?'" In his bid for his party's nomination for the presidency, during a whistle stop campaign across Nebraska, Senator Robert F. Kennedy repeatedly used Shaw's quote. He had a vision, so should you. Still not convinced? Try this one: If you build a better mousetrap, they will beat a path to your door. Remember, if you build it, they will come.

An item of history in the development of marketing as a business discipline was recently reported by the Kellogg School of Management's Marketing Department:

> The eminent marketing historian, Robert Bartels, in discussing the beginnings of marketing thought, points out that the Midwest had the most pronounced influence upon the early development of this field, and that Northwestern University was a major contributor to this effort. Walter Dill Scott, director of the psychological laboratory and later president of the university, wrote *The Theory of Advertising*, in 1903. This book was one of the earliest applications of psychology to this area of business. In 1922, Fred E. Clark wrote *Principles of Marketing*, which established him as a pioneer in the fundamental literature of marketing. Professor Clark was one of the founders of the National Association of Teachers of Marketing and was elected the first president of the American Marketing Association. His reputation extended beyond academic circles into business and government, and his last assignment was as a staff economist to the United States Senate Subcommittee on Trade Policies.

So, while the concept of marketing has been around in America since the turn of the century, there is a general consensus that those of us who attempt to practice marketing know little about it. Traditional marketing focused on products and on the sale of products and services. Little regard was given to what happens before or after the sale. *Sales* was marketing and *retailing* was advertising.

Starting in the 1990s, a new stage of marketing emerged called relationship marketing. The focus of relationship marketing is on a long-term relationship that benefits both the company and the customer. The relationship is based on trust and commitment, and both parties tend to shift their operating activities to be able to work more efficiently together.

Rule of Thumb:
One of the most prominent reasons for relationship marketing is the idea that it costs about five times more to obtain a new customer than to maintain the relationship with an existing customer.

Sales in relationship marketing should encompass the following: open communication, employee empowerment, customers in the planning process, and teamwork. First, communication is essential in figuring out what the customers need and determining how the business can satisfy those needs. With open communication, both sides can express what they are trying to do and can work out a way to make it work together. Second, employee empowerment is important so that the employees are able to satisfy customer needs. Without empowerment, they may be limited in their solutions and cannot creatively satisfy needs. Third, customers must be involved in the planning process. Customer input is invaluable, as the customer is the one who will be using the product or service. If the customer is not satisfied from the beginning, there is no way to gain approval after the product is delivered or the service provided. Lastly, relationship marketing must emphasize teamwork. Several people who can help solve customer problems should work together and use their talents to best serve the customers.

While relationship marketing is considered as the most recent stage of marketing, there is evidence that we are now entering into a new era of marketing called the social/mobile marketing era where companies are connected to customers 24/7. More about this dynamic evolution later.

Chapter 2
Market Research

Since you were in grammar school, you've been fascinated by how computers work and how to fix them. Now, you have decided to open your own small business for computer repairs. Fortunately, your parents have agreed to let you set up shop in the basement to save money and "test the market." Already, friends, neighbors, and schoolmates have come to you with their specific computer repair needs. Being young, you are excited about starting your own small business and seeing it grow. Your best friend has suggested you call it "The Computer Doctor – We Make House Calls."

You know a lot about computers and what makes them work, but not much about the people who buy and use them. One of your teachers challenged you to collect all the information you can on your potential "customers" so you can make the best decisions and get The Computer Doctor off with a good start. These are some of the questions you should be able to answer:

- How many computers are in a typical household?

- What is the frequency of use for each computer?
- What is the average age of a frequent user?
- How much education has the average user achieved?
- What are more common—laptops or desktops?
- What are the best-selling operating systems?
- What are the most common software programs installed?
- How often does a user upgrade to a newer model or version?
- For what purpose do most users buy a computer?
- What is the percentage of different e-mail applications used?
- Do users take their laptops when they travel?
- How do users generally feel about technology in their lives?

If the customer "niche" or target is the home-based computer population, then it is important to find answers to all of the above questions—and more that come to mind as the process unfolds. If the business "mix" is going to include both home-based and other small businesses, then an additional set of questions needs to be addressed and answered. Data pertaining to businesses that should be collected include type of business, locations, number of employees, information technology resources, among other facts and information.

Strategically, it may be good advice to our young entrepreneur to focus the computer repair business start-up on the home-based potential. If experience and success dictate, the home-based business can expand into other markets, such as small businesses and professionals.

Where does a small business owner go to find the important statistics, information, and other data needed to make sound business decisions? Generally, **free** information and **paid** data are available. The good news is that volumes of reliable information exist just for the asking, or clicking, on the Internet. Most organizations in the business of data collection, analysis, and publication in easy-to-read formats are eager to share with interested parties.

Resources include:

- National consumer reports
- U.S. Census Bureau
- Product catalogs
- Trade shows
- Magazines
- Web sites
- Surveys
- Interviews
- Library reference materials
- Business journals
- Testimonials
- Direct user feedback and opinions

In today's age of instant information, there is little shortage of facts, statistics, and revealing data, which can be put to use in the ultimate goal of market research: **Know Your Customer**.

Even as you gather this information, which collectively will create a good idea of who your customers are, you should consider your next level of research. Oftentimes, that level requires developing a more specific, in-depth snapshot of your customers.

Beyond knowing where customers live (geographic), and who they are in terms of age, race, gender, income, education, and occupation (demographic), there is a third measure of research that is more subjective, referred to as *psychographic*.

Understanding psychographic traits and applying this knowledge to your marketing strategies can result in the most loyal and stable customer base. Buyers can change their address, grow older, marry and divorce, but most people cannot change who they are.

Through its StrengthsFinder© assessment, the Gallup Organization has identified and validated these traits as "talents." These talents are developed by all of us at an early age and become the values by which our personal and professional lives are lived. Customers may value a product or service for its safety, prestige, durability, or affordability. Knowing which "button" to push in a marketing campaign can produce tremendous success in terms of building permanent customer relationships.

Rule of Thumb:
Data drives the marketing decision.

This process becomes even more important as time marches on. Be prepared for coming generations— your future customers. Values and needs change, and you should be prepared to meet future challenges. You cannot change the past, but you can determine your future success if you act now in the present. Don't be caught watching your customer base diminish as future generations come into the market. Now, in our technology age, cultural changes are vastly accelerated. Fads and fashions change overnight. Don't be left behind standing at the bus stop, while others are booking a flight to the moon. The space age has arrived. Embrace it!

Finally, keep this in mind: Small businesses are considered the backbone of America and are what many financial analysts predict will be the vehicle to drive us out of financial downturns. A few small business stats (according to the SBA in its 2010 annual report) that stick out:

- There are **27+ Million** Small Businesses in the US.
- Between **60% & 80%** of all new jobs created in our country can be attributed to Small Business.

Congratulations! You are in excellent company!

Chapter 3
Branding and Positioning

What is brand? I'm reminded of scenes from one of my favorite American movies, *Red River*; namely, the branding of cattle in preparation for a historic cattle drive along the old Chisholm Trail. Brands were visual symbols of ownership. They depicted in graphic geometric shapes and/or letters the names of the various ranches: The Circle R, The Flying P, and The Two Rivers are examples. The brand message to all who saw it said, "This is mine, and it is separate from the rest of the herd."

The most successful and durable brands like Coca-Cola, Walt Disney, Ford, and Budweiser create a special relationship between the company providing the product and the customer — indeed, the brand becomes the product in the mind of the customer.

"Brand Bonding" results in the customer experiencing a feeling of ownership. Recent television and print commercial scripts have the actors saying, "that's my CVS," "my Sprint," "my Tide." After multiple repetitions and images of people just like us embracing a product, an almost subliminal message becomes imprinted and oftentimes drives the sales decision.

Brand awareness is not just for big businesses. It is of growing significance to the confidence and credibility of small businesses, as well. When people are asked why they buy a certain product they respond by saying, "I've heard about it." Every small business should incorporate a branding strategy into its marketing plan.

Consider creating a "theme line" to accompany and expand your brand awareness to the buying public. A theme line should be a few easy-to- remember words that underscore the mission of your business. Indeed, the theme line should be an offshoot of that mission statement. When designing one, think of it as a permanent statement to be included in all advertising and promotion—whether it be oral, online, or printed. Being permanent, it can be made stronger each year of operation through your marketing tool kit.

Our young computer repair entrepreneur used the theme line "We make house calls." In 1896, founder H. J. Heinz seized upon the slogan "57 Varieties," although he had more than 60 varieties. Today, his company has over 3,000 varieties, but the theme line is still "57 Varieties." Not only has his company endured but also has his brilliant choice of a slogan, which is now over a century old. It is hoped that "We make house calls" will have the same future. I'm sure that many themes come to mind as you think about it:

- "You're in good hands with Allstate."
- "Breakfast of champions."
- "The pause that refreshes."
- "History made every day."
- "Building America."
- "Just do it!"
- "A little dab'll do ya."

Remember to keep your theme line simple—and more importantly, believable. Don't exaggerate. To wit, as diamonds, your theme line is forever!

The concept of *positioning* is in reality your *niche* in the marketplace. Our Computer Doctor chose to position himself in the home-based community—that became his niche. When customers consider using his services, what characteristics or attributes come to mind? One may be convenience, another personal attention. Lower cost may also enter into the buying decision.

Thus, in all promotional actions, the Computer Doctor clearly emphasizes a *convenient, personal, low-cost service*. That is his business niche. The niche can be said to describe the company's *competitive advantage* or *differentiation*. You can differentiate your product or service by referring to the 4 Ps: product, price, promotion, and place. Other differentiating attributes include quality, variety, service, location, employees, and responsiveness. The attributes you chose for your business then establish the fifth P: position.

Examples of successful differentiation and position include:

- Ford: durability, strength, accessibility
- Mercedes-Benz: prestige, quality, dignity
- Walmart: low-cost, variety, customer-friendly
- Armani: fashion, style, excellence, high-cost
- Brooks Brothers: men's business attire, respect, success
- J. C. Penny: convenient, middle-class, affordable
- Barnes & Noble: current selections, leisurely, no sales pressure

Michael Porter, a professor of marketing at Harvard, is considered to be the business community's foremost authority on competition, or *competitive advantage*. Thirty-five years ago, I was fortunate to have attended several of his classes at the Harvard School of Business. It was intriguing to understand that competition is a good thing for business; the forces of healthy competition drive creativity and innovation. A key attribute that provides product advantage is value.

Price can be a secondary consideration in the search for real or perceived value. Low cost is still low cost; however, the brand's reputation and sustainability can be the characteristics that drive the buying decision. A stay at the Ritz-Carleton is certainly more expensive than the nearest Holiday Inn; however, a special occasion or celebration that calls for prestige and luxury may steer the customer to the Ritz.

An intriguing panorama of branding, positioning, and differentiation can be studied in the rise, fame, decline, and later transformation of the Hollywood movie studio system, beginning in the late 20s and into the 40s and 50s. Historically, the Big Five were MGM, Warner Bros., RKO, Fox, and Paramount.

Metro-Goldwyn-Mayer, founded in 1924, sold glamour and sophistication to its audiences. It was the first studio to experiment with Technicolor and boasted that it had more stars than there are in the firmament. The studio fully developed the movie "star" system. MGM's musical extravaganzas are the foundation of its film library.

Warner Bros. was the pioneer of the "talkies" and developed movies that were "socially realistic." It glorified gangsters and was branded "the gangster studio" with such popular stars as James Cagney and Edward G. Robinson. Its movies focused on tough-talking, working class characters, but later produced "melodramas," another name for women's pictures. Adaptation of classic bestsellers was another of the studio's market position.

20th Century Fox was the studio that introduced CinemaScope with *The Robe* and enjoyed great success with that process.

RKO was known as the home of the B-picture, another way of saying that it produced low-cost, low-budget movies. It was fertile training ground for future directors, who would rise to greater success in better-financed studios or perish.

Paramount focused on developing many of the early stars in the industry, and has survived to this day by delivering movies that respond to the changing needs of the movie-going public.

Although not classified with the Big Five, **Walt Disney Pictures** successfully produced popular family-oriented entertainment and became the favorite source of animated cartoon classics—a position that still continues to propel the conglomerate with great financial success and awards by the motion picture community.

Today, independent and contemporary film production companies come and go; however, the American film studio system branding prevails.

We have considered brands, theme lines, and positioning, from which we defined the Computer Doctor's personal business niche of convenient, personal, low cost service, all leading to his competitive advantage. But it is important to remember that this competitive advantage, in a free market system, is also beneficial to the consumer, who benefits from lower prices and better service. Your involvement as a small business owner in the marketing process is vital and necessary for a healthy community and, thus, a healthy business climate.

Chapter 4
Marketing Plans

If you are already in business, stop and ask yourself the following questions:

- What business am I in—what is my product or service?
- Do I clearly understand my market niche or position?
- What are my company's strengths?
- How do I measure success?
- What are my short-term goals?
- Who are my customers?
- Who are my competitors?

If you are ready to launch your small business enterprise, get a copy of the movie *South Pacific* and pay close attention to *Bloody Mary* when she sings "you gotta have a dream—if you don't have a dream, how you gonna make a dream come true?" She is the epitome of a homegrown successful entrepreneur, selling island goods and services to American Seabees on a remote Polynesian island during World War II (her specialty product is grass skirts). Mary's "dream" is her marketing plan, and she implements it with great bravado, resulting in substantial financial gain.

If you've been in business for some time, are you implementing a marketing plan? Do you know what a marketing plan looks like? If you are not achieving your financial goals, it may be an indication that a plan is needed.

A marketing plan need not be a 30-page academic and theoretical document, which probably will sit on a shelf collecting dust. Your plan must be flexible and dynamic, responsive to changing market conditions. However, you do need one—even if it is a one-page summary.

In Meredith Willson's Broadway musical hit *The Music Man*, Professor Harold Hill, played by Preston Foster, develops "The Think System" to teach instrumental band music to the school boys of River City, Iowa. The plot was meant to be a con job, with Professor Hill collecting fees from the townspeople, then skipping town with the money. As the story develops and builds to a finale, much to Harold Hill's amazement, "The Think System" really works, the boys play, the band marches, and everybody's happy. The End.

Before documenting your marketing plan in writing, I suggest you employ a think system of your own and ponder upon the following considerations:

- What is the purpose of marketing—what is my reason for creating a business?

- How will I carry out the purpose—what is my competitive advantage?
- What is my target market?
- What tools will I use to attack the market?
- Am I clear on my niche, position, and the attributes that I stand for?
- Do customers know who I am?
- How much will the marketing cost? Do I have a budget?

In other words, open up your mind to all the possibilities. After you have thought enough, form a process that will enable you to document categories and strategies for inclusion in a plan.

Here is a sample for our young computer CEO:

THE COMPUTER DOCTOR: "We Make House Calls"

Category	Strategy
My reason for existence	To provide residential computer users in Smallville with timely, personal, and affordable repair services.
What sets my business apart from the others	Focus on home computer customers to include delivery of services on-site.
My ideal customer is:	Youth or adults who use home-based computers for personal or work-related purposes and appreciate the technology
What's most important to my ideal customer when they are buying what I'm selling?	Convenience, availability, cost, and personal service after hours.

What I want to accomplish this year	Establish a loyal customer base and vendor resources
The top three things that are going to get me there.	Word-of-mouth recruiting Flyers in nearby malls and shopping centers Discount ad in local paper
How much will each strategy contribute to income?	30% 50% 20%
What will trigger my ideal customer to think of me	Being at home working on a computer project and encountering a problem
Other potential programs to reach my goal.	Radio TV ad Direct mail piece Open house
How much money will I need to get it done?	$15,000

Success! "The Think System" has created a one-page marketing plan summary.

Nonprofit organizations create a marketing plan for every special event—whether it is the annual signature fundraiser, holiday festival, or the new season of arts programming. Planning is essential for the successful achievement of budget goals and the attainment of fundraising targets. Upon board of directors' approval of a special event, a timeline of necessary activities is established and a committee appointed to make it happen. A sequence of steps in the action plan often constitutes the marketing plan.

Steps may include consensus on the following items:

- Event budget
- Date
- Time and location
- Guest list
- Food and beverage service
- Confirmation of VIP guests or speakers
- Program
- Recruitment of volunteers
- Publicity via e-mail or press release
- Invitations via U.S. mail
- Final counts
- The event happens
- Post-analysis

Scheduling of the timeline is strategic. Adequate time must be allowed between milepost targets to assure an expectation of success. Nonprofits become expert marketers, even though they might not be aware that they are following the marketing rules-of-thumb. Nonprofit organizations routinely schedule their special events annually. Thus, over time they develop a consistent process and benefit from outcomes of previous experiences.

The U.S. Census Bureau data is an excellent resource for developing the targets that marketing plans need to address to be reliable and credible. Do you know your target market when launching a product or service in your community through the formation or expansion of a small business? Do you have a reasonable understanding of the following characteristics?

- Age dispersion
- Employment level
- Ethnic mix
- Household size
- Education attainment
- Per capita income
- Gender ratios

If you need help in finding such data, the Census American FactFinder data set can help. The amount and quality of the data have improved dramatically since the 2010 census. The statistics continue to be published and updated in a timely manner.

Go to www.factfinder.census.gov and search for a Fact Sheet for any community in the country. Use the data you need to arrive at a comfort level to build confidence and authority in designing the target base for your marketing plans.

A second useful data set in the U.S. Census Bureau's Web site is called the American Community Survey (ACS) and can be found on the American FactFinder Website. The ACS is an ongoing survey that provides data every year, giving communities the current information they need to plan services. The survey is sent to 250,000 addresses each month, accumulating three million replies annually. In addition to collecting the base demographic data, ACS also asks about social characteristics such as family and relationships, income and benefits, health insurance, education, veteran status, disabilities, where you work and how you get there, where you live, and how much you pay for living essentials.

All this detail is combined into statistics that are used to help decide everything from school lunch programs to new hospitals. This data can also assist a small business in designing a marketing plan for its products and services. Remember that data is the essential ingredients for decision-making. The more you know about your target market, the better your action plan will be in its effectiveness and ability to reach the customer who needs you.

Chapter 5
Cost of Marketing

The tremendously broad communication tool availability is a definite competitive advantage for starting and running a small business in today's information age. You have the freedom to choose the tools that are right for your business. The American advertising industry focuses on glamour and glitz. When we see the multi-million dollar commercial television ads produced for the Super Bowl and the Olympics, of course we are awed and perhaps made to feel small in our own resources. However, we can also gain some inspiration from the bigshot advertisers.

Rule of Thumb:
One rule of thumb says that the amount you spend on marketing per year should range anywhere from 2 to 10 percent of sales, more or less.

The cost of your marketing efforts depends on many factors, including such considerations as:

- How established is your business, or have you positioned yourself successfully? (If no one has heard of your business yet, you should probably spend more.)
- What industry are you in, and what are your priority products or services? (You should have a sense of how much your competitors are spending.)
- How much can you really afford? (Don't spend yourself into a hole, especially today, when there are so many cheap and highly effective Web options to help you promote your business.)

After you've gathered all the business variables and arrived at an annual figure for marketing costs, don't forget about other marketing-related expenses, such as market research, attending functions and trade shows, training yourself and others, and hiring experts to help you with special projects like improving your Web site and beefing up its content. Also, always allow a bit extra for the unexpected under the **Contingency** line item.

Once you have your annual amount, the challenge then becomes one of allocating your budgeted funds in the most economical manner among the many marketing options available to you.

These options include traditional and proven outlets such as:

- Print
- Radio
- Television
- The Yellow Pages
- Direct mail
- Targeted flyers
- E-mail distribution
- Trade show booths

Don't forget that some of the most essential marketing tools today are also some of the most cost-effective, such as your Web site, and social networking sites like LinkedIn, Facebook, and Twitter.

The key when allocating among them all is to start by thinking about exactly whom you want to reach, and what media they're likely to use.

David Scott, author of *The New Rules of Marketing and PR*, says, "It's always best to start with the people you're trying to reach. Most organizations start with their product or their service, but that's an egotistical approach to reaching potential customers." Scott adds: "You have to think, 'Who is it I'm trying to reach, and where can I find those people?' That will help to drive and inform your marketing."

A great thing about your Web site, of course, is that your potential customers have already found you. You have their attention, and what they now need from you is helpful information.

Therefore, it's important to spend time and money improving the content of your Web site and differentiating yourself from the crowd by providing helpful, personal, interesting content, not just cute graphics and word clutter.

For social networking sites, Scott recommends thinking in terms of a cocktail party. How do you act there? Do you like small talk with many people? If so, Twitter may be for you. Or do you prefer in-depth conversations where you get to know a bit more about one or two people? In that case, perhaps blogging is a good way to go. If you're always networking, even at the grocery store, LinkedIn may be a great way to help you gain customers. No matter what social networking tools you use, always keep in mind the quality of what you're writing and the information you're providing.

When getting down to the nuts and bolts of putting dollar amounts into a budget spreadsheet (Excel is the most widely used), think in terms of a 12-month period with the opportunity for quarterly reviews and adjustments. Complete an entire year even though some months may not change much. Consider the following major sections of a preliminary budget:

- **Supervisory/Management Labor Costs:** You may be a one-person business or be lucky to have hired a Marketing coordinator. Make sure that good estimates are made of the projected time to be spent on purely marketing activities and implementing your marketing plan.

- **Investment:** If you need to purchase certain equipment, such as printers, scanners, computers, and office equipment in order to install and operate the "Marketing Department," you should document the acquisition cost in your budget. Also, if you purchase high-cost software to run on your computers, this should be recorded. A new or re-designed Web site should be included in this section of the budget. Be careful with a Web site—they can be very expensive. Begin with an attractive presence and build on subsequent success and outreach.

- **Operating Costs:** Project the types of marketing options you will use for the coming year and estimate their cost. These could be radio spots, TV ads, newspaper ads, direct mail pieces, and Web site maintenance. Use a budget line item for each. Remember to include related expenses such as copying, printing, and postage.

Check back to the Income/Revenue section of the overall budget to see that the marketing costs are in line with the strategy of a "reasonable" percentage such as, for example, 10 percent. Review actual income and expenditures at least on a quarterly basis and make adjustments to the numbers, as appropriate.

Gone are the days when the bellhop met the train with his handcart to wheel the sample cases to the nearby hotel for the traveling salesman, who might tip him 10 cents a case. Although we now have broad communication tool availability, the competition has also kept pace. Knowing how and when to use these modern tools may well mean the difference between success and failure of your business. We now live in a high tech world—be ready and able to take advantage of it. If you don't, your competition may.

Chapter 6
Strategic Thinking

Think GPS. By now we should all be familiar with the benefits of the *Global Positioning System*. It's in the cars we drive, the smart phones we use daily, and in ways in which we are not aware. We can punch in a location or address and be rewarded with a detailed route of how to get to our destination and how much time it will take. Detailed maps and obstruction-avoiding alternate routes are provided. If this sounds like navigating through the implementation steps of a business strategic plan, it is exactly that. First, you have to have a plan.

Initially, strategy was in the domain of the military. Strategy was crucial to invading armies for the successful conquering of enemies, its lands, and its peoples. Likewise, strategy was key to defense against the invaders. Documented strategic planning by Napoleon, Genghis Khan, and General Eisenhower is now studied at military academies. *The Book of Five Rings* was composed in 1643 by Miyamoto Musashi, the famed duelist and undefeated samurai, and is considered the indispensable guide to strategic planning on the battlefront, as well as in corporate boardrooms.

Not every strategic plan results in success or military victory. History records many examples of failure, such as the famed Battle of the Bulge toward the end of World War II when the Germans defeated Allied forces in the <u>Ardennes</u> Mountains of <u>Wallonia</u> in Belgium. For the Americans, with about 840,000 men committed and some 89,000 casualties, including 19,000 killed, the Battle of the Bulge was the largest and bloodiest battle fought in World War II. Historians credit the defeat with Allied overconfidence, preoccupation with its own defensive plans, and a lack of good intelligence.

Thus, what military strategy teaches the small business community, now that strategic planning has become a buzz marketing tool, is this: Use of strategic thinking must be *flexible* with expected *checkpoints* along the way to assess goal achievement. More importantly, the planning targets must be reviewed and revised accordingly.

Contents of a Simple Strategic Plan. A strategic plan should begin with an agreed-upon simple mission statement, while looking at strengths, competitors, and market forces, together with a set of action plans and a budget. Recommended sections of a reasonable plan include:

1. External Situation
2. Internal Situation

3. Capabilities
4. Assumptions
5. Strategies
6. Goals and Objectives
7. Action Plans
8. Budget

The Strategic Planning Cycle. The strategic plan provides a roadmap for the company to follow. The planning cycle is straight forward. Once a strategic plan is developed, it provides the guidebook for day-to-day operations of the company. In other words, execution of the plan is a continual (daily) process, which is monitored on a periodic basis (perhaps monthly or quarterly). Every so often, perhaps annually or biannually, the strategic plan itself is revised. This cycle is shown in the figure below.

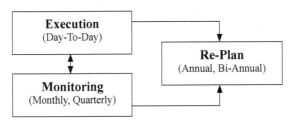

Source: Bradford and Duncan's *Simplified Strategic Planning*.

Having provided a sampling of the more formal aspects of strategic planning, what does strategic *thinking* really mean and how can you use it to enhance your small business profile for the future? Let me give you a brief summary of the *Catalan Strategic Think System*.

First, by now you have a clearer mental image of what your business looks like: its goals, costs, markets, mission, strengths, competitive advantage, and position in the market place. You have also begun the laying of the road map with which your internal GPS will guide you to achieve plan goals. Allow me take a detour and tell you about *Operation Lifesaver*. In 1972, the railroad industry began an educational campaign to teach the public about highway rail-crossing safety. About every three hours, a train in this country hits a person or vehicle. The motto of the campaign is "stop, look, and listen" at rail crossings.

I challenge you to also "stop, look, and listen" every day and reward yourself with a new piece of information about your business and the industry in which it operates. Begin each day with a sense of adventure and discovery—put all your senses on strategic alert.

Where will valuable insights manifest themselves and give you that "aha" moment? Subscribe to a local and a national newspaper; watch the PBS Newshour each evening; get a monthly trade publication; join the Chamber of Commerce, your business association, and the Rotary Club; attend charity fundraisers and dinners; run for public office; become a regular member of your political party; volunteer for community service. Use the networking portion of events to sell yourself and your business. Never run out of business cards to hand out at every opportunity, including the barbershop, the grocery store, and the movie theater.

Create your personalized "Think System" as an integral component of who you are and what you stand for—personally, politically, and professionally. When you do this, you can eliminate the worry about being hit by that train at the next crossing.

Chapter 7
Copywriting

I am going to discuss with you the concept of copywriting in a different context than the legal one with which it is usually associated.

Rule of Thumb:
Copywriting as a rule of thumb is the art of writing advertising copy.

Indeed, copywriting is the bridge linking customers to your products and services in a manner that elicits a response, hopefully, one that results in a sale. Writing well is not an easy task. The need has created an army of successful, highly paid professionals with impressive portfolios and resumes.

But don't worry or tweak that budget upwards. By putting your "Think System" to use and following proven mileposts on that road to achieving marketing goals, you and your team of one or two can shine.

Rule of Thumb:
Shakespeare has contributed a Rule of
Thumb: *brevity is the soul of wit.*

Of course, we all know that achieving brevity is easier said than done. It is much easier to expound and expand when writing than to condense and contract. A fundamental attribute of effective copywriting is to follow the KISS principle—Keep It Simple Stupid. However, besides keeping it simple, you should complete the rule—copy must also be clear and concise. Simple for its own sake can result in simply boring.

When you sit down at the computer to draft a copy for that all-important advertising piece, do not be influenced by your own superior writing skill, rather, you should consider the reader of that copy. Focus on what will turn the reader into a customer. You will want your words to stir and excite, touching "hot buttons." When writing copy, if you develop the unselfish action of taking yourself out of the equation, devote your energy and focus to the potential eyes that will read and react, then you will see results.

In addition to copy that is clear, concise, targeted, inspirational, and influential, there is another critical quality to keep in mind. Good copy should elicit a call to action. Consider the following copy end phrases:

- "Operators are standing by. Call now!"
- "Call in the next 20 minutes and receive a

second set absolutely free."
- "Redeem this coupon for instant cash savings."
- "Everything in the store marked down 20% this Super Sunday."
- "Quantities are limited. Don't delay!"
- "Satisfaction guaranteed or your money back!"

Sound familiar? Have you recently responded to any of these calls to action?

David Mackenzie Ogilvy, an advertising executive, has often been called "The Father of Advertising." In 1962, _Time_ called him "the most sought after wizard in today's advertising industry." He was known for a career of expanding the bounds of both creativity and morality in advertising.

Ogilvy once famously said: "Five times as many people read headlines as read body copy. It follows that, unless your headline sells your product, you've wasted 90 percent of your money." When adding a compelling headline to your ad copy, write the copy first and add the headline last. In this manner, the headline will flow smoother and link itself more dramatically to the copy.

Similar to compelling headlines, are the opening lines in great speeches and novels. Abraham Lincoln's "Gettysburg Address" opens with "Fourscore and seven years ago...." It is as memorable today as when first delivered. Have you ever wondered how memorable his speech would be had he said, "Eighty-five years ago…." Consider the first words of Herman Melville's novel, *Moby Dick*: "Call me Ishmael." Three words that still reverberate in the world of great literature. Or possibly, in your high school English class, you read these opening lines "It was the best of times, it was the worst of times…." from Charles Dickens' *A Tale of Two Cities*. Will your headline be as memorable as these opening lines? Maybe not, but at least now you know the challenge ahead of you. To meet that challenge, you should read great literature, study great speeches, and consult a book of quotations. Each will nourish your mind. President Lincoln attributed his great writing skills to three sources: the Holy Bible, Robert Burns, and William Shakespeare.

My friend, Barbara Shaffer, realized that the Old Market district in Omaha, Nebraska, needed a magazine to promote the area and its various businesses. In 1995, she published the first edition of her monthly magazine, *The Old Market Encounter*; known in the trade as a "niche" magazine; thus, a new small business was created, generating a profit through advertising revenue. Nine years later she sold her publication, which is still being published as *The Encounter* by Omaha Publications, covering downtown Omaha, River Front areas, and the Old Market, while still generating revenue and promoting various businesses through advertisements. Her selection of the name "Encounter" was a stroke of creativity, witnessed by its survival now for 16 years. If it sticks, don't change it. *Encounter* in the masthead of her publication is universal, for it could be used for any city in America to accomplish the same end. As noted above, the present publisher has already included other areas in the city.

The story of Barbara's marketing success was included in this chapter because it is local, personal, and illustrative of entrepreneurship. But it also illustrates the fulfillment of a vision, which is still having a good run. Since her husband, Cliff, was involved in his wife's marketing venture as copy editor, columnist, and feature writer, I have asked him to conclude this chapter in the following paragraphs by providing some tips to further your effort at copywriting, which as previously stated, "Writing good copy is not an easy task."

Neither is providing advice to new, younger generations, who are decades removed from mine. First, you should be bold, for now we are living in the age of an accelerated evolution of language. Although language has always been changing, our high tech world has kicked the pedal to the metal, which brings me to my Uncle Royal, a staid English professor, who I dearly loved, even though he corrected my grammar.

One day I said, "Uncle, how do you like the word 'finalize' that converts the noun 'final' to a verb." To which he simply replied, "Nephew, it is a din upon my ear." But I learned a lot from his attacks on bad grammar as used in good copywriting. One day, to

49

goad him on for the purpose of my further education in good grammar, I mentioned an ad copy that used the words "Healthy Food." He replied, "Nephew, people may be healthy; food may be healthful but never healthy." Unless you're writing your doctoral dissertation, please don't observe Uncle Royal's rules of grammar. The previous sentence was purposely written as an example of clarity versus conciseness, an issue that the copywriter must confront. Uncle Royal's critique would probably be, "Nephew, a dissertation is written for a doctoral degree and a thesis for a master's degree. Be concise!" If you are writing a copy ad strictly for my uncle's colleagues, you would only use the word "dissertation" and be concise, but for a larger population, you should specify the level of academic degree for clarity. Know your audience.

I never told Uncle Royal that copywriters were primarily the guilty culprits who turned his beautiful nouns into verbs. Arguably, the copywriter's crowning achievement of this practice was Kinko's "the new way to office." I believe that their theme song must be Cole Porter's "Anything Goes" from the Roaring Twenties.

Rule of Thumb:
Bad grammar is good copywriting—
depending on the audience.

While it is OK to turn nouns into verbs, it is not right to falsely advertise a service or product. At one point in history, representatives of the United States Marine Corps asked an ad agency to create an ad campaign to increase enlistments featuring in-service training for a future civilian occupation. The ad agency informed them that the Corps lacked such advantages—that pitch belonged to the Army and the Navy. As for the rest of the story, the Corps got their own pitch: "A Few Good Men," concise and appealing.

Ad men live in a world of puns, quips, rhymes, jingles, and anecdotes— with a touch of poetry—a world of words and phrases, which grab the mind and stick. If you publish a magazine, it is copywriting writ large. It's all stories. Stories that will not only entice your subscribers to renew their subscriptions but also will attract new advertisers—the lifeblood of radio, magazines, newspapers, and television. Copywriting writ small must accomplish the same end for your product or service. Whether it is William Shakespeare's *Hamlet* or Ernest Hemmingway's *For Whom the Bell Tolls*, both authors rode the power of the written word to success, albeit a different style, a different time, and a different audience.

Rule of Thumb:
Remember, the only reason a business exists is to make a profit.

If you decide to write your own copy, I suggest that you take a walk, visit a business, and write in your mind copy for that business. Let's visit Vic's Corn Popper in the Brandeis Food Court right here in River City.

Vic's Corn Popper,
A real hunger stopper.
If you're on a diet
You gotta try it.
Popcorn, pop, and yogurt too,
We're here just for you.

Good copy, you be the judge. But hopefully, it has conveyed a method to aid in your copywriting. In my mind, I thought of a rapper performing this ad copy on stage or for a TV slot. Will it sell more popcorn? Don't know. That's the ad business. Now, I'm going for a bag of popcorn. But before taking my leave, I must tell you that Uncle Royal would never approve of the word "hopefully" as used in the second sentence of this paragraph. He would insist on substituting, "I hope." But grammer, schlammer, that shouldn't worry you, a future copywriter.

Chapter 8
Creative Advertising Design

National Geographic Magazine has been published for 121 years and hasn't changed its cover design or format for as long as I can remember. The magazine can be picked out at a distance at any bookstore, newsstand, or other venue where magazines are sold. One of my friends has collected the magazine for the preceding 30 years—they are stacked uniformly in neat rows by date in his basement. Brilliant creative design has sustained the publication through decades of the American and global experience. Upon opening the latest issue, the reader already knows that timely articles illustrated by world-class photographs and graphics will appear upon its pages. I always read the articles and admire the ads from cover to cover. True success.

In 1993, I founded a theater company in Omaha, Nebraska, as a fundraising arm of the Nebraska AIDS Project. Our mission was to create awareness of the AIDS epidemic through the medium of live theater by informing, educating, and inspiring patrons from a cross section of the potential audience base. We titled the enterprise "Support the Nebraska AIDS Project" and graphically created a design banner using the acronym SNAP. We added an exclamation point to differentiate the company from others with SNAP in their names.

***

I'm pleased to report that SNAP! Productions is alive and well and still flourishing in Omaha today. As it grew, it gradually disassociated itself from the Nebraska AIDS Project and incorporated itself as a separate nonprofit organization. Eighteen years later, the appearance of the masthead logo on advertising copy tells readers who have attended SNAP! offerings that a unique theater experience awaits them. The theater company continues to tell stage stories of individuals overcoming bias, isolation, and discrimination, while promoting diversity in very positive settings. I used copy that spoke to "theater as therapy."

In our daily experiences, as we travel the path of personal and professional living, we are constantly called to action by visual and written advertising. Some we automatically file away in some part of the brain created for that purpose, some we take in through a more conscious part of the brain that processes the information, while some force us to stop and marvel at the creativity, which is being revealed before our senses. **Advertising is creativity in action**.

What is creativity? Is it a mysterious quality, like genius, that is present at the birth of each individual? Is it reserved only for the artist, such as a Rembrandt or a Mozart, and cannot flow into the essence of us, who are not blessed with an artistic flair? Why does the use of the adjective *creative* lift the thing being observed into a higher realm of existence? Why does the *creativity* label appear to be out of the reach of most mortals—an attitude that relegates us to a level of just being satisfied with what we assume to be our skills and talents?

Let me assure you that if you are informed, you are creative. Creativity, I believe, is a blossoming of information. The more you know about people and their environments, the greater becomes the understanding of their natures, and "what makes them tick." With such essential acquired information, the better you can appreciate their attributes, and the more expressive you can be in recounting their strengths. On the flip side, the better you know their weaknesses and what to avoid.

Creative ads are designed for the customer with the ultimate goal of a sale and money in the bank for your small business. So it reasonably follows that the more you know about that *potential* or *existing* customer, the greater will be the creative advertising outreach, resulting in greater sales success. The old accolade of the super salesman who "can sell refrigerators to an Eskimo" is a myth—no informed seller would ever try it. You should not answer the question, "Should this action be undertaken?," but rather, "If this action is undertaken, will it have the effect you intended?"

Having systematically and thoroughly conducted market research, knowledge of the customer has become clearer, such as an old Polaroid photo coming into focus before your eyes. By employing "The Think System" you now have your own picture of that customer. Many important details appear, such as:

- Physical appearance
- Normal clothing attire
- Married, single, widowed, divorced
- Lives in a house, apartment, or condo
- Has a spouse and three children
- Works in an office, factory, retail store, or at home
- A young professional, climbing the career ladder
- Middle-aged in the same job for 20 years
- Retired on a fixed income
- Shops for all needs weekly at the local shopping mall
- Watches television twenty hours a week
- Subscribes to three monthly magazines
- Attends a movie alone or with family and friends once a month

The more you know about your customer the longer the list becomes. Adding to the demographic palette of the American population, we also know that there are now more females than males in the country, that the largest immigration sources are Latin America and Asia, and that the elderly are rapidly becoming an influential buying market. Listen to AARP commercials with the tagline: "there are 30 million of us." Recognize this challenge and call to action for your advertising strategy.

When designing an ad for your small business, review the principles of "keeping it simple" and "target the customer." Your first piece will most likely be for a print outlet, such as a flier to be distributed around the neighborhood, in retail stores, shopping centers, and other small businesses within a reasonable radius of your location. If you are our young entrepreneur, "The Computer Doctor," you will want house calls to be both timely and economical. Again, know your customer and stay focused on the profile you have created using "The Think System." The ad is for customer consumption, not your own personal gratification!

To begin implementing your customer orientated marketing plan, which was written with much attention by you and perhaps one or two assistants, you should recognize that budget constraints come into play. A one-page ad in a national magazine, such as *Time*, may cost $90,000 and be designed by an advertising agency. Well, that is an aspiration for the time when "The Computer Doctor" is nationally franchised with offices in most major cities—but not now. For now, you realize that your own personal computer is already loaded with software that will allow you to design a one-page flier. By applying the creativity that has been growing with every new piece of information about your customers, your confidence level in creating a good ad is high. You can now e-mail it to a local copy print shop and pick up the 500 copies you need before the end of the day.

In laying out such an ad, I visualize a page with a "tic-tac-toe" grid across it; that is, three equal sections in three rows vertically and horizontally. It's not a bad idea for beginners to take a blank sheet of copy paper, draw the grid, and then begin to roughly place the essential copy elements within the sections. Copy elements will include information on the business such as name, logo, location(s), hours of business, phone, FAX, e-mail, and Web site address. When describing the product or service being offered, remember to be clear, concise, but compelling. Don't forget that "call to action" tagline. Also, show the product. It can be a stand-alone computer, a computer in its natural setting, as in an office; or a computer in action, that is, in the hands of a user.

Visual and graphic representations can be lines, illustrations, or photographs. Good quality photographs can provide the reader a feeling of intimacy with the product. Lines and illustrations can project movement and action. The "call to action" can be linked to you personally as a business owner with a sincere testimonial. The final draft can then be finessed on the computer, for example, using the Word or Publisher software programs. Use the Internet and other software resources for symbols, clip and word art, type and color of fonts, bold and underlining emphasis, and other accessories to create, at a first glance, an attractive piece. Move the content of the imaginary grid sections around to enhance balance and harmony with the total ad.

White space is the area on the page that is blank; however, do not see white space as a negative. Use that white space to dramatically offset design elements and give them more eye appeal, such as what the mat on a framed painting does for the subject matter. Boldly and subtly experiment with color. Splashes of color on black and white backgrounds may achieve dramatic attention to the copy and message of the ad. Test a final draft with your friends, neighbors, and colleagues. Take their reactions and opinions seriously, always distancing your own prejudices from the task at hand. Reaching out to customers is not about you, but it is about touching a "hot button" in that special customer in a manner that results in positive action.

If you plan to have your inaugural marketing flier printed by a commercial copy print shop, ask to see the first copy that comes off the press. Check it carefully for style, composition, and copy accuracy. Don't hesitate to "stop the presses" for changes or revisions. You want that first message to be memorable and a "keeper" that goes on top of the recipient's "to do" pile of papers and correspondence, not in the trash basket.

I cannot overstress enough that you must definitely decide who is your customer. Many years ago, Standard Oil Company, before it became Exxon, based their marketing plan toward the service station operator as their customer. Following further market research that developed the true customer target was the driver that pulls up to the pump, the company changed their entire marketing and advertising plan.

Neither can I overstress the need to develop catchy, memorable copy and print ads. For many years, a good example of a memorable phrase occurred here in Omaha, Nebraska. On the door of the several Harkert Houses, the very essence of a diner, emphasizing an art deco style, appeared this phrase, "Through these doors pass the most wonderful people in the world—our customers." Or as an eastern donut shop advertised, "Brother, as you go through life heading for your goal, remember to keep your eye on the donut and not on the hole."

A good ad should represent the soul and substance of the business generating it. The potential customer's eyes, upon seeing the ad, should immediately send a message to the brain, transmitting visual images of the physical properties of the product or service. Other senses join in delivering feelings of safety, health, quality, well-being, convenience, and a need to buy and possess the product.

Employ the "art of art" in all your design elements when creating that special ad. Consider the attributes of balance and style to achieve eye-appeal. Every element in the copy, be it a word, a graph, a picture, an illustration, a logo or symbol, or strategically placed white space must be appropriate to the message.

Beyond the lure of traditional print ad advertising, looms the magic of radio and television exposure for your growing business. With initial success and the ability to budget a few more dollars to venture into more exotic advertising media, consider the reach of radio. Radio provides a more intimate approach and can be surprisingly affordable.

With a smart, catchy script, delivered by a voice of authority or sincerity in 15 to 30 second spots and strategically scheduled, the message can likely reach customers in their cars, offices, or bedrooms. Radio time is highly competitive; however, good negotiating skills may be rewarded with a favorable agreement.

Investigate community talk radio opportunities. If your business is in an ethnic neighborhood, such as Asian or Latino, and provides products or services that are unique to their listeners, a local radio station may donate time. Be aggressive in pursuing exposure opportunities. Remember that the message should contain a "call to action."

Of course, for a growing small business the allure of television cannot be denied. Again, begin your campaign for a taste of airtime on a manageable scale. As with radio, community television stations will be receptive to "news" of interest to their listeners. While the reach is on a local or regional frequency, the experience gained can return significant benefits. For a nonprofit small business, investigate Public Service Announcements (PSAs) to reach the public with a special product or service of community benefit. Noon talk shows may be another channel for announcing signature fundraising events. These usually require reasonable advance scheduling. Again, don't forget that critical "call to action." Make sure that airtime includes clear and precise contact information with name and telephone or e-mail address for viewers to respond.

Memorable and sustainable television advertising requires a magic blend of creativity, innovation, stimulating copy, clear voiceovers, eye-catching visuals, and technology. Excellent ads create and engage spokespersons that, over time, and countless viewings, become established icons in your living room or den. Oftentimes, you anticipate their visit. These iconic personalities may be actors, celebrities, or animated creations. They may wear outlandish costumes or behave in unexpected but entertaining ways. *Think Ronald McDonald, Mother Nature, Mr.*

Clean, Tony the Tiger, Smokey the Bear, and *The Jolly Green Giant.*

My good friend, John Prouty, was my roommate for a few months while his permanent residence was being remodeled. A telling component of this experience was the "preferred" television viewing options to be shared. My imbedded, personal preference were movies on the Turner Classic Movies cable network later into the evening. John's TV block of time was in the late afternoon, after a day of creative labor at his graphics company. His favorites were "Jeopardy!" and anything on the Food Channel.

My arrival at the apartment we shared, after a day of nonprofit networking and grant writing, usually occurred in the middle of Rachel Ray's Thirty Minute Meals, or Paula Dean's southern, down-home, comfort food creations. On a number of occasions, becoming visibly and emotionally inspired by whatever food concoction stirred him, John would rush to the market, secure necessary ingredients, and return to prepare the evening meal from memory or instructions he had meticulously documented on paper. Dear Reader, this is a prime example of a successful "call-to-action."

Interestingly, the Food Channel hosts are the product themselves. What is the Food Channel selling? Certainly not food! Successful network chefs become celebrities and make a lot of money. They write cookbooks, endorse products, and rise in the public eye through promotional tours, cooking contests, and guest appearances. The value to the network is the celebrity status of their "stars." The more famous they become, the more viewers tune in to see them in action, and the more money the network makes through sponsorships.

Employ your "Think System" and crank up those creative juices when arriving at the point in your small business growth when you can budget for a television ad. Most likely, it will be modest, but think strategically. You may give birth to a television message in words and visuals that compels viewers to consider your products or services. Consider a focal, iconic visual that elicits a "call to action."

Rule of Thumb:
Consistency is the key to long-lasting ads.

By all means, be consistent. You will know when you have a hit on your hands. You've followed the guidelines, tested the market, created that one-of-a kind advertising print ad or other media spot that has returned your investment in it many times. Your friends, vendors, neighbors, colleagues, and competitors have all commented on your advertising genius. Do not get a big head and start changing everything. Stick with it. Let that one ad define your market niche and what you stand for.

I live in Omaha, Nebraska, in a section of downtown called **The Old Market**. The Old Market is in a historic district, revitalized with some of Omaha's best restaurants and boutique shops. It has been a lively and busy destination since the 70s. One of my favorite restaurants was the *Neon Goose*, a friendly, comfortable, contemporary gathering place serving high quality food and specializing in fish dishes. Unlike steaks, fish is not a prime staple of our local cuisine.

The restaurant was tremendously successful, especially on weekends when folks from around the region made loyal pilgrimages in anticipation of a unique culinary experience. In fact, so successful that the owners made a strategic decision to re-locate to West Omaha, where all new development was headed accompanied with much wealth. The end of the story is that the new *Neon Goose* was forced to close after experimenting with new menus, décor, and a complacent "we have arrived" attitude. Loyal patrons who made the trek to the new, improved eatery found that while the name was the same, the experience was totally alien. The new location was in an upscale, boutique-style shopping center as opposed to the Old Market, which had remained bohemian in keeping with its Old Market atmosphere. In the new location, evening traffic dropped off dramatically. The owners had assumed that re-locating to a more affluent neighborhood would expand their patron base and generate more profit. Wrongly, they transformed the old business into a completely new one without strategically considering the consequences. The old

Neon Goose space, empty for many years, has recently been revived as a nightclub. Good luck!

I'm sure you understand the moral of that story. If you've got a good thing going, stick with it. Enough said.

Chapter 9
Public and Media Relations

It doesn't matter what they say about you as long as they spell your name right.

—*Anonymous*

It's show time in our marketing journey! Time to tell your story. Sell your product. Sell yourself. It's time to practice the art of *public relations*.

> **Rule of Thumb:**
> Simply put, public relations is the art of actively building relationships among the individuals and groups whom you consider to be your publics.

Those publics could be your stockholders, investors, customers, members, employees, and the broader community. If that sounds too simple, consider your behavior with your immediate family members, close friends, and colleagues. How do you nurture and grow those interpersonal relationships. I suggest that a common thread is *communications*.

In his 1967 Oscar-nominated role as *Cool Hand Luke*, Paul Newman plays a prisoner refusing to conform to authoritarian rule and confinement. The movie includes one of Hollywood's most famous and memorable lines spoken by management, represented by Strother Martin as the Captain. After successive hole-digging and refilling harassment, he finally says, "What we've got here is ...failure to communicate." Within the context of the film, the phrase is meant to send a clear message to Luke; namely, that it can be nothing more than a matter of Luke failing to understand the one-way nature of the communication that is incumbent on his present demotion in social status. Use of the phrase is prevalent in today's business and professional environment. Have you used it?

Public relations, abbreviated as **PR**, primarily concerns enhancing and maintaining the image for businesses, non-profit organizations, events or high-profile people, such as celebrities and politicians. Public relation skills are used to build rapport with vendors, customers, investors, employees, or the general public. Almost any organization or business that has a stake in how it is portrayed in the public arena employs some level of public relations.

The practice of public relations is widely spread. On the professional level, there is an organization called <u>Public Relations Society of America</u> (PRSA), the world's largest public relations organization. PRSA is a community of more than 21,000 professionals that works to advance the skill set of public relations. PRSA also fosters a national student organization called Public Relations Student Society of America (PRSSA).

In the USA, professionals working in public relations earn an average annual salary of $50,000. Top earners bring home around $90,000 annually, while entry-level public relations specialists earn around $30,000. Corporate, or in-house communications, is generally more profitable, and communication executives can earn salaries in the mid six-figures, though this only applies to a fraction of the sector's workforce. The role of public relations professionals is changing because of the shift from traditional to online media (discussed in Chapter 10). Many PR professionals are finding it necessary to learn new skills and to examine how social media can impact a brand's reputation.

There are various tools that can be used in the practice of public relations. Traditional tools include press releases and media kits, which are sent out to generate positive press on behalf of the organization. Other widely used tools include brochures, newsletters, and annual reports. Increasingly, companies are utilizing interactive social media outlets, such as:

- Blogs:

A **blog** (a blend of the term *web log*) is a type of Web site or part of a Web site. Blogs are usually maintained by an individual with regular entries of commentary, descriptions of events, or other material such as graphics or video. Entries are commonly displayed in reverse-chronological order. *Blog* can also be used as a verb, meaning *to maintain or add content to a blog*.

Most blogs are interactive, allowing visitors to leave comments and even send messages to each other via widgets on the blogs; It is this interactivity that distinguishes them from other static Web sites.

Many blogs provide commentary or news on a particular subject; others function as more personal online diaries. A typical blog combines text, images, and links to other blogs, Web pages, and other media related to its topic. The ability of readers to leave comments in an interactive format is an important part of many blogs. Most blogs are primarily textual, although some focus on art (art blog), photographs (photoblog), videos (video blogging or vlogging), music (MP3 blog), and audio (podcasting). Microblogging is another type of blogging, featuring very short posts. As of February 2011, over 156 million public blogs were in existence.

- Social media—the most popular being:

Facebook is a social networking service and Web site launched in February 2004, operated and privately owned by Facebook, Inc. As of July 2011, Facebook had more than 750 million active users. Users may create a personal profile, add other users as friends, and exchange messages, including automatic notifications when they update their profile. Facebook users must register before using the site. Additionally, users may join common-interest user groups, organized by workplace, school or college, or other characteristics. The name of the service stems from the colloquial name for the book given to students at the start of the academic year by university administrations in the United States to help students get to know each other better. Facebook allows any users, who declare themselves to be at least 13 years old, to become registered users of the Web site.

Twitter is an online social networking and microblogging service that enables its users to send and read text-based posts of up to 140 characters, informally known as "tweets."

Twitter was created in March 2006 by Jack Dorsey and launched in July of that year. Twitter rapidly gained worldwide popularity with 200 million users as of 2011, generating over 200 million tweets and handling over 1.6 billion search queries per day.

LinkedIn is a business-related social networking site. Founded in December 2002 and launched in May 2003, it is mainly used for professional networking. As of March 22, 2011, LinkedIn reports more than 100 million registered users, spanning more than 200 countries and territories worldwide. The site is available in English, French, German, Italian, Portuguese, Spanish, Romanian, Russian and Turkish. LinkedIn has 21.4 million monthly unique U.S. visitors and 47.6 million globally. In June 2011, LinkedIn had 33.9 million unique visitors, up 63 percent from a year earlier and surpassed another popular networking site, MySpace.

***

One of the most popular and traditional tools used by public relations professionals is a press kit, also known as a media kit. A press kit is a folder that consists of promotional materials that give information about an event, organization, business, or even a person. Usually, included are backgrounders or biographies, fact sheets, press releases (or media releases), media alerts, brochures, newsletters, photographs with captions, copies of any media clips, and social mediums. With the way that the industry has changed, many organizations may have a Web site with a link, "Press Room," which would have online versions of these documents.

For the business community, large or small, working daily at creating a positive image has become increasingly more of a priority. It is now considered a good business practice. Accidents happen. Trains derail. Pipelines rupture. Dangerous chemicals leak. Strange things explode.

Developing strategies to address such unplanned

catastrophes fall under the public relations branch of *community relations*. This area encompasses the wider community in which a business operates, extending to the homes of its staff and employees. Reaching even wider may include the community services, which all persons associated with a particular business or organization use, such as schools, churches, shopping centers, and municipal or government facilities. For nonprofit organizations, establishing partnerships with compatible charitable organizations can build a powerful base of support for fundraising and donor relationships.

During my 27-year employment with the Union Pacific Railroad, I held the position as director of Community Relations for a couple of years. While the staff consisted of a part-time administrative assistant and me, my boss was fond to declare that: "50,000 U.P. employees were available resources to enhance community relations." Indeed, the company at that time ran train operations from Council Bluffs, Iowa, across Nebraska, Wyoming, Utah, Nevada, California, Idaho, Oregon, and Washington. I was based at headquarters in Omaha, Nebraska.

Essentially, my job was to build and maintain positive relationships with the communities through which the railroad operated. Gone were the days when the railroad was the primary economic player in the towns it created as it built its rail system across the western states. The modern transcontinental giant now sped through most of these towns at speeds of 50 to 70 miles per hour, stopping only at strategic fueling stations and crew change locations. Now the trains blocked crossings, where frustrated vehicle drivers waited for mile-long freight trains to pass. Now, train whistles sounding at all crossings within residential and business districts of every town and village kept people awake and alert to a constant fear of a mishap.

All complaints came to me for resolution. I came to know by first name many mayors, city managers, and city council members. I made courtesy calls on city leaders whenever I traveled in their jurisdictions. I attended public dedications and grand openings. I introduced myself to local United Way agency directors and staff.

Through the Union Pacific Foundation the company continues to make financial grants to eligible nonprofit organizations in the communities where Union Pacific operates. This is a major strategic component of the company's community relations plan. When approved, local company representatives personally distribute grant checks and encourage the media through press releases to publicize the goodwill generated. Community outreach is greatly enhanced by the company's philanthropic policy of supporting United Ways, thus distributing financial resources to hundreds of charities in addition to those directly and individually reached.

The company actively encourages its employees to

attend fundraising community and nonprofit events, many times reimbursing attendees for any admission or ticket fees incurred. In addition, U.P. supports the selection of its employees to serve on nonprofit and municipal boards of directors with an implied permission for administrative help during the terms of such service.

This brings us to another important feature of the public relations landscape—*employee relations*. The often-quoted axiom "our employees are our most valuable asset" should be incorporated into the strategic plan of every enterprise and organization. Effective and frequent employee recognition programs can have an immediate impact on the bottom line.

Examples of employee recognition strategies include:

- **Employee of the month.** A posted photograph with caption is enough to generate goodwill among staff. Some companies include a gift or financial stipend and an informal award ceremony.
- **Birthdays and Births**. A modest greeting card sent through the mail with appropriate congratulations makes the employee feel part of a caring family structure.
- **Years of Service.** A pin, plaque, or certificate at five-year anniversaries symbolize significant achievement.

- **Acts of Heroism or Charity**. A gift certificate may be appropriate to award an employee who performs an outstanding personal act or service such as a rescue or assistance to those in need.
- **Community Volunteer Service**. Many companies support their employees by allowing in-house campaigns for membership recruitment and fundraising special events for nonprofits, such as United Way.

Rule of Thumb:
Encourage publicity for outstanding employee activities through press releases and items in company newsletters and other publications.

Media relations involves working with various media for the purpose of informing the public of an organization's mission, policies and practices in a positive, consistent, and credible manner. Typically, this means coordinating directly with the people responsible for producing the news and features in the mass media. The goal of media relations is to maximize positive coverage in the mass media without paying for it directly through advertising.

Many people use the terms *public relations* and *media relations* interchangeably, however, doing so is incorrect. Media relations refer to the relationship that a company or organization develops with journalists, while public relations extend that relationship beyond the media to the general public.

Dealing with the media presents unique challenges in that the news media cannot be controlled—they have ultimate control over whether stories pitched to them are of interest to their audiences. Because of this, ongoing relationships between an organization and the news media are vital. One way to ensure a positive working relationship with media personnel is to become deeply familiar with their "beats" and areas of interests. Media relations and public relations practitioners should read as many blogs, journals, magazines, and newspapers as possible that relate to one's practice.

Working with the media on the behalf of an organization allows for awareness of the entity to be raised as well as the ability to create an impact with a chosen audience. It allows access to both small and large target audiences and helps build public support and mobilizing public opinion for an organization. This is all done through a wide range of media and can be used to encourage two-way communication.

The most effective way to develop meaningful media relations is to get to know the people in the media: editors, writers, reporters, and announcers. They are professionals doing the best job they can; people just like you and me—not glorified celebrity untouchables. The media folks feed on news and stories of interest to the community at large. Certainly, in the course of running your business and employing the "stop, look, and listen" strategy, you become aware of or create something of substance that is newsworthy. Call or e-mail a reporter whose articles you have read that seem to be in tune with your business mission. Depending upon time sensitivity, make a date for coffee or lunch. Begin to build that personal relationship. It will pay wonderful dividends.

Chapter 10
Online Marketing

The traditional and classical strategies and methods of Marketing to our publics, especially our customers, have become less effective as technology continues to transform how we communicate. As you built your small business and reached out to your markets through radio, direct mail, print advertising, and perhaps some minimal television, you became much better acquainted with your customer. Even some interactive e-mail campaigning brought you closer to understanding customer needs and aspirations.

We find ourselves today in an age of some truly transformational and dynamic changes going on regarding the way marketing fits into our business plan. Just ask yourself a basic question: "When I shop for things, how do I find them?" If you answered, "I turn to Google," then you are in the 80 percent or of folks who do just that. The reason I mentioned Google as the search engine is because more people use it than any other search database/engine. For your business to be found on Google, use your personal "Think System" and pretend you are Google. How does

Google think?... Think Internet.

Internet marketing is inexpensive when examining the ratio of cost to the reach of the target audience. Companies can reach a wide audience for a small fraction of traditional advertising budgets. The nature of the medium allows consumers to research and to purchase products and services conveniently. Therefore, businesses have the advantage of appealing to consumers in a medium that can bring results quickly.

Internet marketers also have the advantage of measuring statistics easily and inexpensively; almost all aspects of an Internet marketing campaign can be tested, traced, and measured in many cases through the use of an <u>ad server</u>. The advertisers can use a variety of methods, such as *pay per impression, pay per click, pay per play, and pay per action*. Therefore, marketers can determine which messages or offerings are more appealing to the audience. The results of campaigns can be measured and tracked immediately because online marketing initiatives usually require users to click on an advertisement, to visit a website, and to perform a targeted action. However, from the buyer's perspective, the inability of shoppers to touch, to smell, to taste, and "to try on" tangible goods before making an online purchase can be limiting. However, there is an industry standard for e-commerce vendors to reassure customers by having liberal return policies as well as providing in-store pick-up services.

Think *inbound marketing* when designing strategies for your Web presence. In other words, design your Web site so that the content attracts users to it.

 Rule of Thumb:
Website content is king.

Take innovative steps to assure that your site is one that customers will want to visit because they know that valuable and timely information is contained in it. They will know that their questions will be answered and that solutions to their individual problems will be solved.

Again, think consistency. Stay with the principle of "the customer first and foremost." Persistent consistency will reward you. Customers will eventually be predisposed to choose you for their needs. Remember that you must be current and relevant. Consider publishing a regularly appearing blog on your Web site so the interactivity enhances your customer appreciation and your bottom line.

Be generous. As the volume of visitors to your site increases because you are now a credible problem solver and provider of valuable content, you will find yourself building links into your site. By all means, encourage it. Customers who link to your site will love you. This activity will create enhanced authority with Google and begin to move your site closer to the top when users try to find you. A quicker find gets more traffic to your site.

Rule of Thumb:
Remember: popping up on the second page of a Google search result means certain online death.

I'm reminded of a pivotal plot line in the move *Miracle on 34th Street* when Kris Kringle, played by Edmund Gwenn, alias Santa Claus, begins to refer customers to Macy's arch rival Gimbels for merchandise not available at Macy's. Kris' boss, Maureen O'Hara, fires him; however, the action backfires when Macy's experiences an army of loyal customers due to the goodwill created by the referrals. A new, creative marketing "gimmick" becomes a win-win profitable outcome for both Macy's and Gimbels, not to mention their customers.

While I'm not predicting a repeat of a Hollywood-inspired marketing fantasy resulting in huge profits, I can assure you, by generously allowing external links on your Web site, good things will happen.

What can I say about *social media*? It is here big time. Embrace it. Focus initially on the "big three" I previously introduced: Facebook, LinkedIn, and Twitter. Establish yourself in these and aggressively begin to build a following.

When using Facebook:

- Remember to be open and honest and use the name of your company for your Fan page. Social media is about being *real and personal,* so be sure to follow through in that way.
- Try to use some graphics or at least your logo on the page. It is difficult to do much else, but try to make your page distinguishable from all the others.
- There is a little room to put in a short description about your business; be sure to use it and remember to link back to your page.
- Remember to promote your Facebook account with a "Follow us on Facebook" link on your Web site.
- Here are some best practices for using Twitter:
- Twitter offers more options to personalize your site than does Facebook, so be sure to include your company logo, short description, and a link to your site.
- Start Tweeting. It will take a little while to get some followers, but stick with it and look for people who are in your business space or seem to be searching for whatever it is that you do or sell.
- Get out there and engage with people. Your prospective clients are talking about things that your business addresses. You need to search for these keywords within Twitter in order to

root these conversations out, then add value by responding with helpful suggestions and ideas or tips.

- Remember to add value rather than to self promote. In fact, it is important to remember that this notion is at the core of creating any content in social media or on your site or blog. Do not self promote! People can smell a sales pitch a mile away and will shy away from you—try to help them in a genuine way and they will become interested in what you and your business have to offer as a natural consequence.

- LinkedIn is more of a professional networking tool than a way to directly promote your business. Here are some suggestions for its use:

- Create a LinkedIn group that has something to do with your business. Groups are simply collections of members with a common interest that communicate in discussions about those interests. From your home page just look for the Groups menu and start one up.

- Include your blog and Twitter feeds on your LinkedIn home page.

- Go to the Answers menu item and start answering questions there. You can narrow down your area of expertise by browsing for the appropriate category and focusing

on questions there. Note that you can gain
notoriety the more often your response
is selected as the best one by the author,
thereby establishing yourself in this tool as a
thoughtful leader.

E-mail marketing is one of the oldest and most effective forms of digital communication available. Over the years the technology has become more sophisticated, allowing users to send automatic messages, create beautiful HTML templates, and customize outgoing traffic.

E-mail marketing requires you to follow some rules. The CAN-SPAM Act says that your customers must opt into receive mail, and you must always give them an easy way to opt out.

The easiest way to run e-mail marketing campaigns is with automated software, which is extremely affordable and user friendly. You can use it to send newsletters, coupons, updates, and announcements. Try not to send more than one a week to avoid e-mail overload.

There are many different e-mail marketing providers, the market leader being Constant Contact. They offer an affordable online system aimed at absolute beginners. Integration with social media puts this provider at the top of the list of many satisfied users.

E-mail marketing is an essential piece to the

marketing puzzle. Whether you are a beginner or seasoned professional, there is a provider that can help you succeed.

Chapter 11
Measuring Success

Armed with your dynamic strategic plan and your creative marketing plan, allow yourself a time-out at frequent intervals to "stop, look, and listen" with the goal of critically assessing where you find yourself on your business journey to success. How you measure your success can be an elusive and foggy target. However, clear and expected signposts should appear along the way. If your goals have been SMART ones, that is:

- Specific,
- Measurable,
- Attainable,
- Relevant, and
- Timely,

then that Polaroid snapshot should be coming into clearer focus with background details obvious. If you can put checkmarks next to the following criteria, you are on the path to greater success:

- Organizational and leadership effectiveness
- Staff and employee loyal retention
- Customer base growth

- Community acceptance
- Competitive advantage
- Financial stability
- Income achievement
- Market share potential

If your assessment reveals shortcomings in any of the targeted goals, you may consider scheduling focus group sessions to conduct some problem-solving techniques. Another channel is to design and administer surveys among those publics impacted. Remember to share the results of these initiatives with all participants to assure ownership and commitment for improvement.

Since us business folks love to use acronyms, create a set of SMARTER goals, adding:

- Evaluate and
- Re-do

to demonstrate to your publics that you are serious about taking action on the feedback from group discussions and surveys. Some of your public relations action steps relative to planning may appear to be symbolic to the general public; however, keep the confidence and trust of close colleagues and allies intact. Take action. Post your planning actions and results on your Web site in the form of quarterly reports from the company CEO in an informal, "fireside chat" format and invite reader comments and suggestions for further improvement.

Rule of Thumb:
Keep in mind that a critical strategy
of quality management is continuous
improvement.

Do not miss any opportunity to communicate any significant product or service enhancements, breakthrough innovation, or industry recognition to your publics and to the media.

I live in a historic, renovated, eight-story building in Omaha. This building is now owned by the Sentinel Real Estate Corporation, which is based in New York. It was built in 1905 as a warehouse for the storage and distribution of pharmaceuticals. In the 1970s, it was converted to apartments and named "The Greenhouse" for its distinctive series of spaces housing three-sided glass enclosures where the former huge freight elevator made its frequent runs up and down the north wall of the building.

Four exceptional people manage this 129-unit property by practicing each day the craft of relationship marketing. Monica, the general manager, is assisted by Stephanie. The maintenance "twins" are Brian and Mike. The four come together to function as a team, operating as if they were a massive army.

The operating environment of The Greenhouse lies in the neighborhood of Fortune 500 companies, such as ConAgra Foods and the Union Pacific Railroad.

Therefore, competition among the several nearby residential apartment and condominium buildings is high. The Greenhouse measures its success in the sustained percentage of leased apartments, which is consistently at 100 percent, with a waiting roster of future tenants.

The concept of business relationship marketing that accounts for success is truly unique and creative. Such partnerships, with major local employers, afford their employees substantial discounts as residents. Called the Preferred Employer Program, it has been a model for others to emulate. Residents are made to feel as if they live in a quality hotel with an on site *concierge* 24/7. Lease renewals are accompanied by apartment upgrades in the form of new décor, appliances, and carpet replacement or cleaning. Consideration is given to resident requests. Deliveries are made to the residents' doors. Mail can be held during absences.

Thus, for The Greenhouse success is not simply the enviable 100 percent leased statistic. It is the goodwill generated through a commitment to meeting and often times anticipating customer needs.

Chapter 12
Build a Future Market

I conducted an unofficial survey among my friends, colleagues, and small business owners for purposes of this book. I asked them to respond in one sentence to the question "What is Marketing?"

Here are some of the responses:

- "Successful marketing is salesmanship in many forms and mediums, based on thorough understanding of the product or services and the best target buyer." —Hal Daub, Law Partner
- "Marketing is a work of art." —Ed Dale, Real Estate Mogul
- "Marketing is presenting your business offerings to the public and your audiences." —Patrick Minikus, Small Business Owner, Laundromat
- "Marketing=selling." —Kris Queen, Small Business Owner, Custom Blinds
- "Marketing is all the means involved in promoting the customer benefits to your target market." —Dave Craig, Laundry Equipment Distributor

- "Marketing is everything that happens, whether you had anything to do with it, that makes people want to participate in whatever it is you're doing." —Val McPherson, Community Volunteer
- "Marketing" is the act of tapping into the conscious (or subconscious) of your audience by communicating a message that resonates deeply and inspires feeling or action." —Leslie Kuhnel, MPA, Community Member
- "Know your market before you start marketing, reaching out to the wrong customers is a waste of energy and money." —G. Leitch, business owner
- "Marketing is what has to happen before anybody is even aware of the new online course that I have spent weeks researching, designing and developing." —Megan Seymour, Senior Instructional Developer
- "The malingering of media and product designed to entice, coerce, cajole or manipulate the mind to make decisions favorable to the media and product." —Thomas Scharlow, Automobile Service Consultant
- "Marketing, to me, is broadcasting your product or service relentlessly to everyone you can possibly reach out to during your every waking moment and loving it." —Van Deeb, Author/Speaker/Salesman

- "Marketing is selling yourself, your business, your ideas, your organization in a manner that reflects the integrity of the product." —Arva Herman, Executive Director, Service Club
- "Marketing is something that salespeople use to sell us things that we don't want or need." —Chris Hanna, Hispanic Chamber of Commerce

While these marketing statements may seem to vary among the respondents, we can ascertain common threads taken as a collective whole. I note action verbs such as: sell, know, promote, research, broadcast, understand, and communicate. These are all powerful words containing strategic direction for the small business owner who incorporates these strategies into his personal tool kit for success.

What does the future hold for the world of marketing? Unlike television's so-called psychics of the 1950s and 1970s, notably *Criswell Predicts* and the *Amazing Kreskin*, who became international celebrities by predicting everything from earthquakes to UFO visits, we are bound by reality today.

At the risk of appearing to be full of myself, I feel compelled to introduce to you a preview of the future, compliments of "Catalan Predicts." This exercise combines the benefits of using "The Think System" and "stop, look, and listen" on a daily basis:

Rule of Thumb:
More intimate interactivity will
characterize the new marketing.

If you call Domino's Pizza to order delivery service more than once, the company's combination of innovative technology and customer service trained personnel is expressed in greeting you by name, confirming delivery address, and remembering special preferences. The transaction may take less than 30 seconds, unless you are put on hold due to the increased volume of orders. Plus, delivery is guaranteed to happen in less than 30 minutes.

If you are a Netflix customer, their computer system keeps track of your movie selections and builds a profile of what you like in film genres. The system makes recommendations for your consideration and quickly adds them to your lineup for future shipments if you simply click to choose. In Omaha, where I live, receipt and delivery is a one working day transaction, accompanied by an e-mail confirming receipt and shipment. A rating program enhances the computer's uncanny ability to make future choices for your approval.

Built into more than 30 GM models, OnStar keeps you safely connected while in your vehicle. OnStar services include automatic crash response, navigation, roadside assistance, and hands-free calling. I cheerfully pay the affordable monthly fee for my Chevrolet Impala after I had to call OnStar when my car's power suddenly departed on a snowy January morning. From the initial, "Mr. Catalan, how may I help you?" to the arrival of a tow truck 20 minutes later, I felt that OnStar was my new best friend.

I buy most of my books online from Barnes & Noble. Even though I've never met any of their service representatives personally, they are my friends. My profile is maintained in their computer system. I'm greeted by name when I log in to order, an activity that takes less than a minute. The book arrives within five working days to my door — sooner if I pay an additional convenience express fee. Personal e-mail notification of my order receipt and shipment is made. Frequently, I receive discount coupons for future orders.

Rule of Thumb:
Future personal messaging from online suppliers will introduce animated visual "people" appearing on the computer screen to take your order interactively.

Digital and physical worlds will combine to engage the consumer in advertised products. Companies can now be in constant communication with their consumers, whether in print, on TV, online or via mobile phones. The hugely successful Old Spice ads featuring "<u>The Man Your Man Could Smell Like</u>" are an example of a recent campaign that began on TV and became an online phenomenon. The commercial, which features a funny script delivered by a man with chiseled abs, has been watched online by millions.

Marketers have also gotten creative about providing opportunities for physical interaction with their products. For example, Mitsubishi developed an online test-drive that allowed potential customers—sitting at home—to control an *actual* car driving around a track.

Following the digital revolution, many advertising agencies are looking for similar ways to bring the digital and physical worlds together. It is a new and future trend.

 Rule of Thumb:
Quick Response (QR) codes will replace the traditional bar codes.

 A QR code can store text and multimedia in a small square pattern. They are appealing to small business owners because the technology is free and readily available. To the left is the QR code I created for my business.

QR codes have been popular in Asia (read Japan) for years, and are just beginning to pop up in the United

States. They can be found in magazines, newspapers, grocery store ads, maps, invitations, and business cards. They are easy to create (trust me—I did it!) and can be scanned with a smart phone equipped with a camera and QR code reader application. To get a code do a Google search for "QR Code Generator." There are now hundreds of online services that let you create QR campaigns, and the majority of these sites are100 percent free to the user.

You can create many different types of QR codes for your business. Some of the more popular ones are:

- Simple text,
- Go to URL (your Web site),
- Send an e-mail,
- Send an SMS text message, and
- Download contact information.

QR codes are a simple, cost effective way to promote your business and keep customers engaged. Try it with a simple message—you will feel a huge sense of accomplishment!

Rule of Thumb:
No longer optional, social media is a must for small businesses.

Jumping on the social media bandwagon is a must! It is not just a fad; small, medium, large, and gigantic businesses are all adopting social media in order to interact with customers, get feedback, increase exposure, and build brand awareness.

Consumers are beginning to look at social media presence as a sign of success and will be more likely to trust you—not to mention be more likely to come in contact with your brand, leaving your name at the top of their awareness the next time they are in search of your product or service.

If you have not already, sign up and create an account for each of the top three: Facebook, LinkedIn, and Twitter. Investigate others, such as StumbleUpon and FourSquare, after you've had some good experiences and need to expand your social network.

 Rule of Thumb:
Unexpected service providers will emerge from non-traditional sources.

In the August 14, 2011, Sunday morning edition of the *Omaha World-Herald*, my one and only hometown newspaper, is a full-page color ad, which reads in part:

Small business owners: Grow your business with a professionally designed website.

The *Omaha World-Herald* is introducing another great product designed for our small business customers. Increase your presence on the web and social media with a professionally designed, cost-effective website from the *Omaha World-Herald*.

• Web hosting and site development

- Choose one of our three web packages—Gold, Silver or Bronze— to best suit your needs and budget
- Custom email addresses
- Video, social media and mobile options
- **The first 25 businesses to sign up will receive free promotion introducing their new websites to our readers.**

Why is this advertisement significant? It shows a negative future that challenges the print media industry, while also demonstrating what one business is doing to strategically meet that challenge to the benefit of small businesses. The Audit Bureau of Circulations, which tracks all newspaper and magazine subscriptions, reports average weekday circulation at 635 newspapers declining by 10-20 percent over the past two years. The assumption is that readers are migrating to the Internet and to Web-based online newspaper editions to get their daily dose of news, good or bad. This trend is confirmed by other tracking agencies. Intrinsically, we know that to be true. Personally, I discontinued my daily paper delivery, staying only with the Sunday edition (working the Sunday crossword puzzle is my favorite therapy session). On a daily basis I quickly check the online editions of my own local paper, *The New York Times*, and *The Wall Street Journal.*

A great deal of talent is contained within the typical

newspaper infrastructure. Strategically, a newspaper enterprise keeps up with state-of-the- art technology in writing software, graphics arts design, copywriting skills, computer and printing equipment—all with a culture of getting things done quickly. What more creative manner to use excess capacity than to offer it to small businesses.

Rule of Thumb:
Big business partnerships with small business will blossom.

The big supermarket where I do most of my necessary and impulse grocery shopping offers "fuel points" for each dollar expended. Customers are offered a unique ID card, which can be added to your keychain to track purchases. In partnership with a chain of small convenience stores across the company's playing field, accumulated fuel points may be "cashed in" for gas—each 100 points equals ten cents off the fuel cost, up to a maximum of 1,000 points, or one dollar off the pump per gallon price.

This is a brilliant *competitive* advantage strategy! In today's rising food and fuel costs, the program is a total success. Everybody wins, and the customers' loyalty, primarily to the supermarket, soars.

Omaha is the hub for several national insurance companies. One of the larger ones built its own printing facility to handle increasing volumes of print materials distributed by mail to existing and potential customers. The economic upturns of the 70s and 80s created enough new business to justify such a costly capital expenditure. With new technologies, corporate downsizings, and streamlining of the paper processing system the printing facility began to see a decrease in its workload. Added to this development, of course, was the increasing amount of business transacted online through the Internet.

This particular company began as a family business with a strong commitment to employee relations. As an alternative to the layoffs of employees at the print shop and possible retirement of a huge asset in shop presses and other equipment, it found a solution in keeping with its mission of being a "good corporate citizen" to its community. The company announced through the network of nonprofit organizations a new program: It would print materials for eligible nonprofit organizations at cost plus. Those of us who have worked in the nonprofit sector know that the search for low cost or donated design and print services of brochures, pamphlets, annual reports, invitations, and fundraising materials is a major undertaking, but definitely necessary when working with limited financial resources. Thus, the partnership developed by the big insurance company and the smaller nonprofit community is a tremendous example of creative solutions that result in mutual benefit.

Does your small business have a product or service that could be of economic benefit to a larger business? Think about it. As big business continues to downsize and outsource, there may be a role for you to play as an independent contractor. Be proactive and consider your opportunities upon hearing about companies spinning off divisions and unprofitable operations.

Timeline of significant events in history, which impact the field of advertising and marketing today and tomorrow.

- 1450: Gutenberg's metal movable type, leading eventually to mass-production of flyers and brochures
- 1730s: Emergence of magazines (a future vector of niche marketing)
- 1836: First paid advertising in a newspaper (in France)
- 1864: Earliest recorded use of the telegraph for mass unsolicited spam
- 1867: Earliest recorded billboard rentals
- 1880s: Early examples of trademarks as branding
- 1905: The University of Pennsylvania offered a course in "The Marketing of Products"
- 1908: Harvard Business School opens
- 1922: Radio advertising commences
- 1940s: Electronic computers developed

- 1941: First recorded use of <u>television advertising</u>
- 1950s: Systematization of <u>telemarketing</u>
- 1970s: <u>E-commerce</u> invented
- 1980s: Development of <u>database marketing</u>
- 1980s: Emergence of <u>relationship marketing</u>
- 1980s: Emergence of computer-oriented <u>spam</u>
- 1982: The Internet is introduced
- 1984: Introduction of <u>guerrilla marketing</u>; e.g. an unconventional system of <u>promotions</u> that relies on time, energy and imagination rather than a big <u>marketing budget</u>.
- 1985: <u>Desktop publishing</u> emerges
- 1995: The <u>Dot-com bubble</u> re-defines the future of marketing
- 1996: Identification of <u>viral marketing</u>; e.g. <u>buzzwords</u> referring to <u>marketing</u> techniques that use <u>social networks</u> to produce increases in <u>brand awareness</u> or to achieve other marketing objectives (such as product sales).
- 2004: Facebook is launched
- 2006: Twitter is created
- 2010: U.S. Census is taken with enhanced data collection

Bibliography
Books and Periodicals

Bartels, Robert, *The History of Marketing Thought* (3rd. ed.), Columbus: Publishing Horizons, 1988

Kaiser & Mitilier, *Rule of Thumb*, Omaha: WriteLife LLC, 2010

Levitt, Theodore, *Levitt on Marketing*, Boston: Harvard Business School Press, 1991

Levinson, Jay Conrad, *Guerrilla Marketing*, Fourth Edition, New York: Houghton Mifflin, 2007

Muckian, Michael, *One-Day MBA in Marketing*, Paramus: Prentice Hall Press, 2001

Oglivy, D., *Oglivy on Advertising*, Toronto: John Wiley & Sons, 1983

Porter, M.E., *Competitive Advantage*: New York: Free Press, 1985

Porter, M.E., "Strategy and the Internet", *Harvard Business Review*, March 2001

Slutsky, Jeff & Marc, *Smart Marketing*, Franklin Lakes: Career Press, 1998

White Papers

Get Busy Media, *5 (Easy) Ways to Energize Your Marketing*, 2011

Inbound Market Link, *The 10 Essential Steps to Effective Marketing Online*, 2010

Intuit 2020 Report, *Twenty Trends That Will Shape the Next Decade*, 2010

Author Biography

David Catalan is the president of Catalan Consulting. Prior to establishing his consulting practice in April of 2008, he was the executive director of the Nonprofit Association of the Midlands from August 2002 to February 2008.

David served as a cabinet member in the office of the former mayor of Omaha, Hal Daub, during the last year of that administration in the capacity of director of Workforce Development for the City of Omaha. Before that he was executive director of the Omaha Press Club, a private membership organization promoting excellence in journalism and press relations.

Prior to joining the Press Club, David was on the administrative staff of Metropolitan Community College for three years. He managed the areas of marketing, public relations, finance, planning, staff development, and facilities as vice-president of Finance and Administrative Services. During his tenure there, the Workforce Development Institute was established.

David Catalan came to Omaha from Los Angeles in 1980 with the Union Pacific Railroad and served with the railroad in a variety of positions, including government affairs and community relations until 1993 when it was reported erroneously that he had retired. As you can see, that is not the case.

David has a master's degree in Business Administration from Pepperdine University and has attended the Harvard Business School Program for Management Development, the Alliance Francaise in Paris, and the English Institute in Heidelberg.

He served in the military during 1960-1966 in California and Indiana, as well as in Germany and France.

David's civic and community involvement is quite extensive. He is a founder of El Museo Latino in South Omaha. He has served a governor-appointed position on the Nebraska Arts Council, as a board member of the Omaha Community Foundation, the Douglas County Health Department, and the American G.I. Forum of Nebraska. He is president of the South Omaha Business Association.

Clients of Catalan Consulting include the Mexican American Historical Society of the Midlands, which he helped to incorporate in 2009, the Small Business Association of the Midlands, the Latino Caucus of the Nebraska Democratic Party, and the recently opened Omaha Classic Coin Laundry in South Omaha. Specialty areas include training, fundraising, strategic planning, and organizational development.

Made in the USA
Middletown, DE
13 July 2021